GEARED FOR GROWTH BIBLE STUDIES

GOD PLANS FOR GOOD

A STUDY OF JOSEPH

BIBLE STUDIES TO IMPACT THE LIVES
OF ORDINARY PEOPLE

Christian Focus Publications

The Word Worldwide

Written by Dorothy Russell

PREFACE
GEARED FOR GROWTH

Where there's LIFE there's GROWTH:
Where there's GROWTH there's LIFE.'

WHY GROW a study group?

Because as we study and share the Bible together we can

- learn to combat loneliness, depression, staleness, frustration, and other problems
- get to understand and love each other
- become responsive to the Holy Spirit's dealing and obedient to God's Word
and that's GROWTH.

How do you GROW a study group?

- Just ask by asking a friend to join you and then aim at expanding your group.
- Study the set portions daily (they are brief and easy: no catches).
- Meet once a week to discuss what you find.
- Befriend others, both Christians and non Christians and work away together
see how it GROWS!

WHEN you GROW ...

This will happen at school, at home, at work, at play, in your youth group, your student fellowship, women's meetings, mid-week meetings, churches and communities,
you'll be REACHING THROUGH TEACHING

INTRODUCTORY STUDY

'From My Postbag'

(1) Dear Chris,

I'm just so shocked and numb, I don't know how to tell you about the terrible thing that has happened. I came home from our Sunday School teachers' meeting and found a note from Jim saying he felt our marriage had finished. He's gone – left me and the children.

Although he didn't mention it, I know that Mrs S., a deserted wife from the next street, has subtly influenced him to make this decision. She's very clever and pretty, and Jim has always admired her. We've tried to befriend her as she seemed so much alone.

I know our marriage wasn't perfect, but I loved Jim. I just feel shattered at the thought of living without him. What can I do, Chris? Please help me. – Jan

(2) Dear Chris,

I didn't think I'd ever need to ask you this, but something I read in my Quiet Time the other day made me feel a tinge of guilt, so I decided to share it with you. At work, 'D' and I seem to be thrown together a lot, as he and I are working on the same project. I find that I am beginning to look forward to these times quite a lot, as I enjoy his company and he always makes me feel terrific. Once or twice lately when we've been alone, he's said things that could be taken two ways. I've felt my heart beat faster!

Of course, I'd never do anything 'wrong', but I am only human and we all need to feel accepted. I am troubled by some of my thoughts, especially when alone. You see 'D' is a married man.

Please advise me, as I want to do the right thing. – Pat

(3) Dear Chris,

I feel I just can't cope with life any longer. Although I'm a Christian, everything seems to have gone wrong lately. Nothing works out for me and I've begun to get so depressed. My friends don't understand what I'm going through, and the doctor only gives me another prescription for tablets.

If only I didn't get so 'down', I might get through to God and He would help me, but this depression seems to go on and on, and I can't see any way out. Perhaps there isn't any way out. – John

(4) Dear Chris,

Gwen and I have worked hard for years to buy what we own. We are proud of our new home. At last the children have plenty of space. We have two cars, and on weekends we like to visit our shack and do some fishing or skiing. Of course, we bought the boat with the Church young people in mind, and we sometimes ask them to join us.

Now that times are easier for us and I get more time to think, I realise that deep down I don't have the satisfaction I expected. Surely it's not wrong to be comfortably off and be able to give the family some pleasure?

What's the answer to the emptiness in my life? – Bill

(5) Dear Chris,
Could you please give me the address of another Bible Study group in my area?

Mrs J., has recently started to attend our study and I can't feel happy with her in the group. (The problem goes back years now and is too deep-seated to overcome.) I feel it's better if I just move out without causing any more hard feelings. – Meg

* * * * *

God sometimes allows us to be tested with the kind of problems these people faced. They might be labelled:

(I) The test of adversity   (Gen. 37:28)
(2) The test of the body   (Gen. 39:7)
(3) The test of the soul   (Gen. 40:I5)
(4) The test of prosperity   (Gen. 4I:4I, 42)
(5) The test of the inner man (Gen. 50:I9-2I)

Joseph went through all these five tests during his life.

THE FAVOURED SON	RESPECTED IN EGYPT	TEMPTED BY POTIPHAR'S WIFE	MADE GOVERNOR OF EGYPT	OPPORTUNITY FOR REVENGE

THE VICTIM OF OTHERS'
ENVY AND WRONG DEEDS

WRONGLY ACCUSED
LEFT IN PRISON FOR
TWO YEARS

How did he cope? He learned:
(a) That he could trust God in **every** situation, because He is Sovereign.
(b) That God was with him in every situation, and gave him strength to 'pass the test'.

Do you see your problems as stumbling blocks – or stepping stones into a deeper walk with God?

STUDY 1

QUESTIONS

DAY 1 *Genesis 29:16-31; 30:22-24; 35:16-19.*
Make a family tree, showing Joseph's parents and his brother.

DAY 2 *Genesis 21:1-3; 25:19-26.*
a) Add to the family tree Joseph's paternal grandparents and great-grandparents, and his uncle.
b) Genesis 35:23-26. Now list his 10 half-brothers.

DAY 3 *Genesis 30:1-26.*
Try to put yourself in Rachel's situation. How would she have felt:
a) before she became pregnant,
b) after Joseph was born?
c) What affect would this probably have had on Joseph?

DAY 4 *Genesis 32.*
Joseph would have been about six years old at this time.
a) What things recorded in this chapter would he have witnessed?
b) What new name was given to his father?

DAY 5 *Genesis 33:1-20.*
a) What was the reaction of Joseph's uncle when he met Jacob?
b) Where did they camp at this stage of the journey?

DAY 6 *Genesis 35:9-20, 27.*
a) What happened near Bethlehem, which would have been the first major tragedy for young Joseph?
b) Where did the family arrive?

DAY 7 *Romans 8:28.*
a) Think back over your own life. Have you caught any glimpses of how God has been working out His plan for your life, in the situations you have been in?
b) 1 Corinthians 6:9-11; 2 Timothy 3:15. From what contrasting backgrounds does God call people to be His children? From which do you think Joseph came from?

NOTES

The Bible is very honest when telling the life stories of its great men and women. We read about their struggles and their shortcomings, their fears and their very human failings.

Jacob and Rachel, Joseph's parents, are not portrayed as paragons of virtue; instead we see them as normal human beings, like ourselves, who sometimes do things they are ashamed of later. We also read of their firm faith in God and because of this God was able to work in their lives and in the lives of their children.

Rachel prayed long and earnestly for a son, and God gave her her heart's desire. Isn't it reasonable to suppose that she prayed for that boy from the moment she knew he was to be born? Those of us who are parents, grandparents, aunts, uncles, or godparents have a special responsibility in prayer. Are we fulfilling this God given task adequately?

Jacob may have started off as a liar and a deceiver, cunning and intent on getting his own way, but when he met God face to face at Peniel, he became a changed man. The Bible says, 'If any man be in Christ, he is a new creation'. Can you look back to a time when you became a new creation in Christ? God wants to have complete control of your life so that He can, as time goes on, change you into His likeness, and fit you to live with Him eternally.

And Joseph ... born into this rather mixed-up family clan, experiencing a long, arduous and sometimes frightening journey at a tender age, then losing his mother, to whom he was everything ...

What of him?

We have the rest of the study to find out! And I think it will be very interesting.

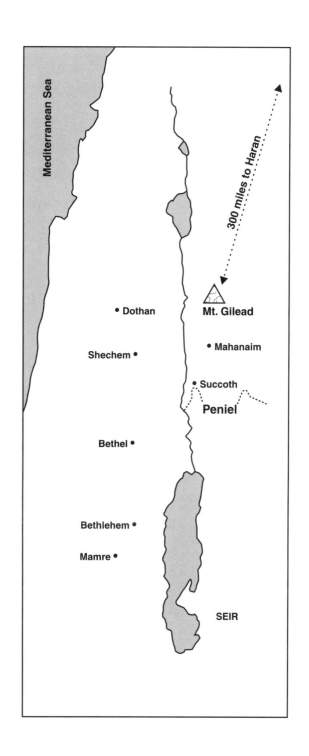

QUESTIONS

DAY 1 *Genesis 37:1-4, 9-11, 31-35.*
a) What can you find out about Joseph's father from these verses?
b) Is there a warning to those of us who are parents?

DAY 2 *Genesis 37:4-11.*
a) Which verses give us the reason for the ten brothers' attitude to Joseph?
b) If there is anyone of whom you are jealous, tell the Lord about it. What should we do to overcome this sin (Jas. 3:14; 1 Pet. 2:1)?

DAY 3 *Genesis 37:2; 35:25-26; 33:2.*
a) Who had acted wickedly?
b) What cause had they to hate Joseph?

DAY 4 *Genesis 34:24-31; 49:5-7; 37:12-20.*
a) The sordid story recorded in chapter 34 took place at Shechem. Find it on last week's map. How would you describe the brothers Simeon and Levi?
b) Which verse in chapter 37 might have been spoken by them?

DAY 5 *Genesis 37:21-24, 29-30; 49:3-4; 1 Chronicles 5:1.*
a) Why would Reuben be particularly jealous of Joseph?
b) What part did Reuben play in the story?

DAY 6 *Genesis 37:25-28; 49:8-10; Matthew 1:2-3.*
a) How did God use Judah to save Joseph's life?
b) What special promised privilege was given to his descendants?

DAY 7 *Genesis 37 (or read verses not already read in this chapter).*
a) What age was Joseph when he was sold as a slave?
b) What do you think his feelings were as he: told his dreams, went to find his brothers, lay in the pit, was sold as a slave.

NOTES

How quickly Joseph's fortunes changed! And don't forget he didn't know the end of the story, as we do. As far as he was concerned, this **was** the end; slaves didn't often live very long, especially if they had cruel taskmasters.

If you have ever been plunged into a situation of hopelessness and despair, seeing no way out, with the dull monotony of life never getting any better – you may have some idea of how Joseph felt.

If you have had a crushing tragedy in your life, a shock from which there seemed no recovery, an end to all your hopes and ambitions – you will know something of the torturous sorrow that must have engulfed Joseph.

If death or sickness has separated you from one you loved dearly, and you feel life will never be the same again – just think of Joseph trudging the weary miles, longing for home and happiness, and thinking, 'If only this hadn't happened!'.

> But this was *not* the end of the story.
> Nor is any trouble, however great, the end
> of the story for God's child.
> This was the Test of *Adversity*.
> What can we learn from Joseph?

Acts 7:9 says, 'Because the partriarchs were jealous of Joseph, they sold him as a slave into Egypt. But God was with him.

God was with him – did he realise this?
God has promised that He will never, never forsake His children.
God was in complete control, Joseph had only to hang on in faith, God was moulding Joseph's character to become like that of His dear Son. God says in His Word that He will not allow anything to overwhelm us, which, with His help, we are not able to bear (I Cor. 10:13).
God loved Joseph, and was allowing him to go through this dreadful experience as part of a greater purpose.

Years later, Joseph was able to say to his brothers:

'You intended to harm me, but God intended it for good to accomplish what is now being done, the saving of many lives' (Gen. 50:20).

STUDY 3
RESISTING TEMPTATION

QUESTIONS

DAY 1 *Acts 7:9-10; Genesis 39:2, 3, 21, 23.*
a) What thought is common to each of these verses?
b) What came about as a result of the Lord's presence?

DAY 2 *Genesis 39:1-6; 1 Corinthians 10:31.*
a) How do these two readings complement one another?
b) Think of something you have to do, which you don't like doing. Try applying the principle of 1 Corinthians 10:31, and share with the others what happened!

DAY 3 *Genesis 39:6-12.*
a) Which verse tells us that this temptation Joseph had to face was persistent?
b) Why did Joseph realise that to give in would be such a wrong thing?
c) Read Proverbs 7:6-27 and compare the two situations.

DAY 4 *Genesis 41:38; 1 Corinthians 6:15-20; 1 Thessalonians 4:3-8.*
a) How was Joseph able to resist this temptation?
b) What advice would you give to a friend who is tempted to have a wrong relationship?

DAY 5 *Genesis 39:13-19; James 3:5-12.*
a) One sin leads to another. How did Potiphar's wife add to her guilt?
b) Which verse from the 'James' reading do you find most significant? How can this reading relate to the Joseph story?

DAY 6 *Genesis 39:20-23; 1 Peter 2:18-23.*
a) According to the Bible, what should our attitude be if we have to suffer for something we didn't do?
b) How was it evident to the other prisoners that there was something different about Joseph?

DAY 7 *John 19:1-11; Isaiah 53:7-9.*
a) What impresses you most about these accounts of the sufferings of Jesus?
b) How can this help you in your daily life?

What do you do when you have a problem?
Two courses are open to you:

ACCEPTANCE or RESISTANCE

Joseph's first problem in Egypt was a situation that he could not change – slavery in Potiphar's house. Here God indicated that He required humble *ACCEPTANCE*. Not easy? No, indeed, for Joseph had been the favourite son of a wealthy man, and pride must have been one of his early characteristics. Yet the one thing that enabled Joseph to *ACCEPT* his situation, was his overwhelming desire to put God first in his life, and to do *everything*, every menial task, to God's glory. He would have agreed with Paul, who said, 'So our aim is to please him always in everything we do' (2 Cor. 5:9 LB).
RESISTANCE would have been quite wrong in this situation.
Joseph's next problem was temptation. Potiphar's wife made repeated efforts to seduce him as he went about his daily work.
Here was a situation that Joseph could change, but it needed all the courage he could muster. Here, he saw quite plainly that God required *RESISTANCE*. This was the *Test of the Body* (see Introductory Study). How did Joseph manage to *RESIST* this temptation? Again, it was his overwhelming desire to put God first in his life, and with God's help he saw this woman's suggestion for what it was – SIN.
Have you ever thought how the whole story of God's purposes for His people would have been changed if Joseph had blotted his copybook at this stage? *ACCEPTANCE* would have been quite wrong in this situation. I Corinthians 10:13 (RSV) says:

'God is faithful, and he will not let you be tempted beyond your strength, but with the temptation will also provide the way of escape.'

God's 'way of escape' this time was prison, but at least in prison Joseph was safe from the scheming wiles of an unscrupulous woman.

ACCEPTANCE or RESISTANCE

We need wisdom to know which course to take when confronted with problems in our daily life.

'God grant me serenity to accept the things I cannot change,
courage to change the things I can,
and wisdom to know the difference.'

STUDY 4

PRISON

QUESTIONS

DAY 1 *Genesis 39:20–40:8.*
a) What is the most important thing about Joseph in this section?
b) What responsibilities did Joseph have while he was in prison?

DAY 2 *Genesis 40:8-15; Ephesians 3:1; Philippians 1:13.*
a) What request did Joseph make to the chief cupbearer (butler) after he had told him the meaning of his dream?
b) In what way was Paul's imprisonment similar to Joseph's?

DAY 3 *Genesis 40:16-23; Psalm 62:1-8.*
a) Imagine yourself in Joseph's situation. What feelings would you have as you talk to these men? How would you feel during the two years of chapter 41:1?
b) What did the Psalmist find best to do in time of trouble?

DAY 4 *Genesis 40:8; 41:16; Daniel 2:26-28; Acts 16:9-10; Numbers 12:6-8; Hebrews 1:1-2.*
a) What clues can you find here about God's use of dreams given to:
  – heathen kings?
  – His own people?
b) What are the more usual ways in which God communicates to His people today?

DAY 5 *Genesis 41:1-8; Proverbs 20:24; Romans 8:28.*
a) What things did God use for Joseph's good at this point?
b) Describe the first dream in your own words.

DAY 6 *Genesis 41:9-16; Psalm 105:16-22.*
a) How God tested Joseph's patience! Could God not have made the butler remember sooner?
b) Why did He not? (The clue is in the Psalm.)

DAY 7 *Genesis 41:17-27; Psalm 105:17.*
a) What was the meaning of Pharaoh's dreams?
b) What was God's reason for giving Pharaoh these dreams?

NOTES

This section can be a tremendous help to anyone suffering from depression, mental trouble, or from Satan's attack on the mind in any way.

Look up the diagram in the Introductory Study again.

We are now studying the 'Test of the Soul' – sorrow, sickness, suffering, in the face of which we cry,

'Why?' 'Why has it happened to me?' 'What have I done to deserve this?'

And the only answer that comes back is *'Trust Me.'*

If you are experiencing any mental anguish at present, there is much you can learn from Joseph. What did he do in this dreary, soul-destroying, seemingly never-ending situation?

1. *He remembered that God was with him.*
You may feel you have lost contact with God – remember, He *never* loses contact with you. Satan's line is always to make us doubt God. Remember the Garden of Eden?

2. *He accepted the situation, trusting God to work it out.*
This is not the same as resigning yourself to a life of misery! It is a patient waiting and looking ahead with hope and confidence that God does all things well. Without this acceptance, a person can become bitter and frustrated.

3. *He occupied himself as best he could, doing faithfully what he was able.*
You may long to do things which are impossible for you at present, but be thankful for the small things you can do, and do them cheerfully.

4. *He was concerned for others whom the Lord brought across his path.*
Satan tries to make you believe that no one is as badly off as you are! You look at others who are 'on top' at present, and down you go into the mud of self-pity. Yet because of what you are going through, God may be able to use you to help someone else.

5. *He bravely bore the long waiting time,* though there seemed to be no hope and no one who cared about him.

One of the most devastating things in a time of suffering is not knowing how long it will go on. But God knows and He will give you strength to endure, and victory over your feelings of self-pity. Remember, He has something precious to teach you through this suffering.

STUDY 5

QUESTIONS

DAY 1 *Genesis 41:28-36; Psalm 107:33-35; 1 Kings 17:1; 18:1.*
a) What do these readings teach us about God?
b) What plan did Joseph suggest to Pharaoh?

DAY 2 *Genesis 41:37-38; Luke 4:16-19; Ephesians 5:18.*
a) What do you think caused Pharaoh to make this remark about Joseph?
b) Share with the group some occasion on which you felt the leading of the Holy Spirit.

DAY 3 *Acts 6:1-3; Galatians 5:22-26.*
a) Why was it important for the seven men in the 'Acts' reading to be full of the Holy Spirit?
b) In the lives of Christians you know, what fruit of the Spirit do you see?

DAY 4 *Genesis 41:39-44; Acts 7:9-10; Matthew 6:33.*
a) This change in Joseph's status may make you think of a character in the New Testament. Who?
b) How does Joseph's life to this point bear out the truth of the 'Matthew' reading?

DAY 5 *Genesis 41:45-46; Luke 3:23.*
a) What effect might this newly acquired prosperity have had on Joseph at this age?
b) In what ways do you think affluence might be hindering your growth in the Christian life? Write down one practical thing you can do to correct this.

DAY 6 *Genesis 41:45-52; 48:1-5.*
a) During the seven good years, what further blessings did God grant to Joseph?
b) Later, what great promise did the old man Jacob give to Ephraim and Manasseh?

QUESTIONS (contd.)

DAY 7 *Genesis 41:53-57; Matthew 25:23; John 2:1-8; John 6:30-35.*
a) How does God reward those who are faithful to Him in the everyday things of life?
b) What parallels can you find here between Joseph and the Lord Jesus?

NOTES

What a change in Joseph's fortunes! In a matter of hours he had been taken from a sordid prison and exalted to be second only to Pharaoh, the king of that vast, wealthy land of Egypt at the height of her glory. How easily this could have gone to his head!

God's fourth test was:

THE TEST OF PROSPERITY

Can we in the Western world deny that we are prosperous, compared with the millions of underprivileged?

Can you look back to a time when you were not so well off materially as you are now? If you can, humbly thank God, but also BEWARE!

If we could interview some of the Bible characters we have met during our Bible Studies, we might ask them this question: 'Do you think there is anything wrong with a Christian having all that he or she can afford of material possessions, considering the affluent society in which we live?'

MOSES: 'And when the Lord your God brings you into the land ... to give you, with great and goodly cities ... and houses full of all good things ... and when you eat and are full, then take heed lest you forget the LORD who brought you out of the land of Egypt' (Deut. 6:10-13, RSV).

DAVID: 'If riches increase, set not your heart on them' (Ps. 62:10, RSV).

AGUR: (Who wrote some of the Proverbs) 'Two things I ask you, O LORD ... give me neither poverty nor riches, but give me only my daily bread. Otherwise, I may have too much and disown you' (Prov. 30:7-9).

HOSEA: 'The people of Israel have built palaces, but they have forgotten their own Maker. The people of Judah have built fortified cities' (Hos. 8:14, GNB).

PAUL: 'But whatever was to my profit I now consider loss for the sake of Christ. What is more, I consider everything a loss compared to the surpassing greatness of knowing Christ Jesus my Lord, for whose sake I have lost all things' (Phil. 3:7-8).

JESUS: 'Do not store up for yourselves treasures on earth' (Matt. 6:19). 'How hard it is for the rich to enter the kingdom of God! Indeed it is easier for a camel to go through the eye of a needle than for a rich man to enter the kingdom of God' (Luke 18:24-25).

Perhaps this is the time for each one of us to consider our attitude to material possessions.

Are 'things' more important to me than God (be honest)? If misfortune struck and I lost all my personal belongings, how would it affect me?

Which would give me the biggest thrill – a new car, or a member of my Study Group committing his/her life to Christ?

Do I need to reconsider how much I should be giving directly to God's work? George Beverly Shea sang:

'I'd rather have Jesus than silver or gold,
I'd rather be His than have riches untold,
I'd rather have Jesus than houses or lands,
I'd rather be led by His nail pierced hands –
Than to be a king of a vast domain
and be held in sin's dread sway,
I'd rather have Jesus than anything
this world affords today.'

God tells us in His Word that we didn't bring any money with us when we came into the world, and we can't take away a single penny when we die (I Tim. 6:7). With that in mind, read the following quotation from a book by Harry Foster:

'The Christian's hope is similar to Joseph's, though infinitely greater. Not in hours, but in a moment he is to be snatched from this sordid world into the glory of Christ's presence. For him, one day will begin as unpromisingly as all the others, but it will prove to be the day of his translation. All this will happen, not by the decree of some earthly Pharaoh, but by the word of the Lord. It may happen very soon.'

STUDY 6
UNRECOGNISED

QUESTIONS

DAY 1 a) Look back to your answer for Day 5 (b) last week. Have you done what you intended to do? Can you share the results with the group?
b) Genesis 42:1-5. This week imagine you are one of Joseph's brothers. What might the mention of 'Egypt' make you think of?

DAY 2 *Genesis 42:4-13; 37:5-8.*
a) What incidents in today's reading might prick your conscience?
b) What impression does the governor of Egypt make on you?

DAY 3 *Genesis 42:14-20.*
a) Describe your feelings and fears as you hear what the governor has to say.
b) Did you notice something this Egyptian governor said, which you might not have expected?

DAY 4 *Genesis 42:21-24; 37:21, 22, 29.*
a) You suddenly realise how frightened Joseph must have felt that day, over twenty years ago. Which verse tells this?
b) Why are you glad it is Simeon and not Reuben who is bound and has to stay behind (see also chapter 49:5-6)?

DAY 5 *Genesis 42:25-35.*
a) Everything that happens on this wretched trip seems to make you more miserable. What is the latest development?
b) What is your reaction?

DAY 6 *Genesis 42:36-38.*
a) How does their father receive the news about the trip to Egypt?
b) Why is he so fearful about Benjamin, when he doesn't mind the rest of you going?

DAY 7 *Genesis 43:1-14.*
a) What arguments does Judah put forward as to why you should return to Egypt and take Benjamin?
b) What is their father's only consolation?

NOTES

This part of the story may seem rather strange. As you have tried to put yourself into the shoes of the guilty ones this week, have you sensed that uncomfortable feeling? That pricking of the conscience again and again?

Haven't you felt this in your own experience? I'm sure every one of us has, at some time, so don't think you're unique! Unconfessed sin is a most uncomfortable feeling. Guilt can torment us in a frightening way and we lose our peace of mind.

Why should God put these brothers through such a time of mental anguish? Was it revenge for what they had done? No, there was a deeper purpose.

Look at the situation.

These ten men were the fathers of the tribes of Israel, God's own people. He had chosen this family, and was going to make them into a great nation who worshipped Him, and through whom His own dear Son would be born into the world.

However, these men had committed a great sin which they had not confessed, and therefore, it could not be forgiven. As time went on, their consciences became dulled, although obviously the guilt feelings were still there. Psychiatrists today realise the dangers of a submerged guilt complex, and do all they can to bring these feelings out into the open and let the person put things right. This is exactly the way God dealt with these men, for their own good and the good of their families.

They had to be:

reminded of their sin,
really convinced of the seriousness of that sin in God's sight,
given the opportunity to repent,
– and then they could be forgiven.

As the story unfolds, we will see God working His purpose out and bringing these men to the point where they are ready to come to Him on **His** terms.

Is anything keeping you back from coming humbly to God and asking His forgiveness? Pride is usually the stumbling block, and until you can get over that, your life will continue to be dark and full of feelings of guilt.

Wouldn't it be much better to experience what this hymn describes?

'Heaven came down and glory filled my soul,
when at the cross the Saviour made me whole.
My sins were washed away.
My night was turned to day,
Heaven came down and glory filled my soul.'

Why wait any longer?

STUDY 7
DEEPLY MOVED

DAY 1 *Genesis 43:15-18.*
a) Think back over the study so far. What lessons have you learned, or what has impressed you most?
b) The brothers have returned to Egypt. What are Joseph's feelings? What are the brothers' feelings?

DAY 2 *Genesis 43:19-26.*
a) Where has Simeon been? How do you think he might have reacted to seeing his brothers again?
b) What were the presents referred to in verse 26?

DAY 3 *Genesis 43:27-34.*
a) Joseph showed his concern for his father. Think of some relative or friend of yours whom you haven't seen for some time. Before next week's study, sit down and write them a letter, ring them up or make contact in some way. What a wave of Christian love will be going out from our study group this week, to people who perhaps feel lonely or forgotten!
b) What do you read about Benjamin in this passage?

DAY 4 *Genesis 44:1-6.*
a) What plan did Joseph put into action at this stage?
b) Can you think what Joseph hoped to achieve by this plan?

DAY 5 *Genesis 44:7-16.*
a) Why were the brothers willing to make the promise in verse 9?
b) In the fresh calamity of verse 12, what thought was uppermost in their minds?

DAY 6 *Genesis 44:17-26; 37:26-27.*
a) The plan unfolds, why did Joseph suggest they might all go free except Benjamin?
b) Contrast Judah's attitude in the two readings.

DAY 7 *Genesis 44:27-34; John 15:13.*
a) Had Joseph's plan succeeded? What had Joseph discovered by it?
b) What link can you see between these two readings?

NOTES

At this point in our story we see the brothers humbled, broken, and casting themselves completely on the mercy of this great and powerful, all-knowing and inscrutable Grand Vizier of Egypt. There was not one shred of evidence they could use in their defence, no merit of their own that they could claim, and absolutely no hope for them unless this man (who was second only to Pharaoh) showed them *mercy*.

Did they remember their father's last blessing before they left home?

'And may God Almighty grant you *mercy* before the man' (Gen. 43:14).

> God is All-mighty.
> All-powerful (omnipotent),
> All-knowing (omniscient),
> Present everywhere (omnipresent)
> The Holy One of Israel,
> The Most High God.

As you come before Him, do you realise that nothing you have done gives you even the right to stand before Him? Because you are a human being tainted with sin you deserve to be excluded from His holy presence? All your righteousness is like filthy rags in His sight?

It is a real blow to our pride when we realise we cannot win favour with God by the way we have lived, or by anything that we have done.

> 'Nothing in my hand I bring,
> Simply to Thy cross I cling,
> Naked, come to Thee for dress,
> Helpless, look to Thee for grace.'

MERCY has been defined in these ways:

The gracious favour of a superior to an inferior, all undeserved.
God's faithfulness, despite human unworthiness and defection.
The steady, persistent refusal of God to wash His hands of His wayward people.

Joseph's brothers were terribly afraid when they cast themselves on the mercy of the great man of Egypt. But the Bible tells us that when we come humbly before Almighty God, simply trusting in what Jesus has done for us, we need have no fear.

When I stand before Thy throne,
Dressed in beauty not my own
When I see Thee as Thou art
Love Thee with unsinning heart,
Then Lord, shall I fully know,
Not till then, how much I owe.'

'Therefore he is able to save completely those who come to God through him'
(Heb. 7:25).
'Let us then approach the throne of grace with confidence, so that we may
receive mercy' (Heb. 4:16).
'God, have mercy on me, a sinner' (Luke 18:13).
'Surely goodness and *mercy* shall follow me all the days of my life' (Ps. 23:6,
AV).

STUDY 8

QUESTIONS

Let us fix our thoughts on JOSEPH this week, for it is in this chapter that we see a man who has come through prolonged suffering and testing, and whose character now shows the fruit of his absolute trust in God.

DAY 1 *Genesis 45:1-5; Hosea 3:1; 1 John 4:9.*
a) What characteristic shows up in Joseph, which reminds us of the character of God?
b) How does Hebrews 2 :11,17 link in with this passage?

DAY 2 *Genesis 45:4-8.*
a) How is Joseph an example to us to heed the warning in Hebrews 12:15?
b) Pick out another characteristic in Joseph which Jesus tells us about in Matthew 6:12-15.

DAY 3 *Genesis 45:4-9; 40:8; 41:16; 50:20.*
a) What was Joseph very sure about?
b) Read Romans 8:28 and 1 Peter 2:21-23, and share any thoughts that come to you.

DAY 4 *Genesis 45:9-15; James 2:14-16.*
a) What does God look for in our lives as an outworking of our faith?
b) How did Joseph put this into practice?

DAY 5 *Genesis 45:16-20; Psalm 25:12.*
a) Consider verses 10 (spoken by Joseph) and 18 (spoken by Pharaoh) in the light of Psalm 25:12. What does this show us about how Joseph made his decisions?
b) Proverbs 3:4-6. Share with the group some time in your life when you put God's will before your own wishes.

DAY 6 *Genesis 45:21-28.*
a) What did Joseph give his brothers to take home?
b) What convinced Jacob that Joseph was alive?

DAY 7 *Galatians 5:22-24; Genesis 41:38.*
a) Which fruit of the Spirit can you see in Joseph's life?
b) Why might you have expected him to produce this fruit?

NOTES

Have you realised that Joseph's attitude to his brothers, after all he had gone through, was only possible because he allowed God to have control of every part of his life? This is the key to producing the fruit of the Spirit.

Check your own life against some of the characteristics of Joseph's life highlighted in the answers to this week's questions and see where you fall short. Now, as a group, join in a time of silent prayer, each one asking God to forgive you for one particular thing, and to help you overcome it.

Our study this week has shown us the *Test of the Inner Man*. Can you remember what the other four tests were? Joseph once more came out on top, trained and disciplined by the hardships or difficulties that God had allowed in his life, and he freely forgave his brothers.

'What amazing love!
Can it really be?
Can our eyes believe
What we seem to see?
Can a man forgive?
Can a man forget?
No, I can't believe it's true–
And yet ... and yet ... and yet ...

If human hearts are often tender,
And human minds can pity know,
If human love is touched with splendour,
And human hands compassion show:
Then how much more shall God our Father
In love forgive, in love forgive.'
(from the musical HOSEA)

If God is allowing you to go through a time of suffering and testing, can you hold on, trusting Him who is able to keep you from falling – as Joseph trusted? Can you say, 'God sent me here'?

If God has blessed you, and has given you much you can be thankful for, remember, He has not done this so that you can sit back and become self-satisfied; God blesses you so that you can be a blessing to others – as Joseph was.

'But God sent me ahead of you to preserve for you a remnant on earth and to save your lives by a great deliverance' (Gen. 45:7).

STUDY 9
REUNITED

QUESTIONS

DAY 1 *Genesis 46:1-7; 26-30; Acts 7:11-15.*
a) How was Jacob reassured that it was right for him to go to Egypt?
b) How many people went to Egypt?

DAY 2 *Genesis 46:31-34; 47:1-6.*
a) Why was it a risk to introduce the family to Pharaoh as shepherds?
b) Where were they allowed to settle? If possible, find this on a map.

DAY 3 *Genesis 47:7-22.*
a) Look carefully at verses 7 and 10. What did Jacob do?
b) List in order the things the Egyptians had to give or sell in exchange for food?

DAY 4 *Genesis 47:23-31; 46:4.*
a) What can we discover about the famine from these verses?
b) Why was Jacob so insistent that he should be buried in Canaan?

DAY 5 *Genesis 48:1-9; Hebrews 11:21.*
a) What promise of God did Jacob remember so vividly (Gen. 28:10-17)?
b) Write down one of God's promises that means a lot to you.

DAY 6 *Genesis 48:10-22.*
a) Who was the younger of the two boys?
b) What did Jacob do that displeased Joseph?
c) With verse 22 compare John 4:5.

DAY 7 *Psalm 105.*
a) With whom did God first make His covenant, or treaty?
b) After Joseph's day, why did the people not want to stay in Egypt?

NOTES

Stand back and take a long view of God's dealing with His people.

When the Psalmist does this, he is overwhelmed with gratitude to God for being such a *faithful* God, faithful to His covenant with His people. Psalms 105, 106 and 136 look back to what God has done for His people over the years, and each one begins with the exhortation to

'give thanks to the LORD'.

When Stephen (Acts 7) was arrested and brought before the Council, his defence took the form of a recital of the history of God's people. This is centred upon God's promise to Abraham (vv. 5, 17) and His faithfulness in keeping His promise, in spite of man's unfaithfulness. Stephen could see God in complete control of history, and he had the courage to proclaim this, even though it cost him his life.

The writer to the Hebrews (in chapter 11) shows how it was the men who had faith, who found real happiness. Even though they died without seeing the promises fulfilled, they believed that what God had said would come true, and this gave them joy and security.

Abraham trusted God, and he obeyed.

Sarah had faith, she realised that God would do what He had promised.

Isaac knew, by faith, that God would bless Jacob and Esau.

Jacob had faith in God's promise, and he passed on the blessing to Ephraim and Manasseh.

Joseph was sure that God would bring His people out of Egypt as He had promised.

How wonderful are God's promises and His plans and purposes! It's good to see where Joseph fits in to the overall picture and how God was able to use this man because he was available to Him.

Where do you fit in to God's plan and purpose for the world today? He guides and directs those who love and trust Him, and who are completely available to Him. Often we can't see why things happen, but we can be like God's people of old, and be unshakeable in our faith in His promises.

'God is working His purpose out as year succeeds to year,
God is working His purpose out, and the time is drawing near,
Nearer and nearer draws the time, the time that shall surely be,
When the earth shall be filled with glory of God, as the waters cover the sea.'

'And we know that in all things God works for the good of those who love him, who have been called according to His purpose' (Rom. 8:28).

STUDY 10

QUESTIONS

DAY 1 *Genesis 49:1-15.*
a) Which of Jacob's sons are mentioned in this passage?
b) Who is verse 10 referring to?

DAY 2 *Genesis 49:16-27.*
a) What other sons of Jacob are mentioned in today's reading?
b) What does Jacob say about Joseph. What had God done?

DAY 3 *Deuteronomy 33:13-17; Ephesians 1:3-8.*
a) What did Moses say about Joseph?
b) What blessings do those who belong to Christ have?

DAY 4 *Genesis 49:28-33; 50:1-3.*
What impression do you get of the old man Jacob (remember he was over 130 years old!) in this deathbed scene?

DAY 5 *Genesis 50:4-14.*
a) Who made up the party to go back to Canaan to bury Jacob?
b) When had Joseph last seen this land?

DAY 6 *Genesis 50:15-21.*
a) Imagine this scene. Why did Joseph weep (v. 17)?
b) Give another example in the Bible of man doing something evil and God turning it into good.

DAY 7 *Genesis 50:22-26; Exodus 12:40-42; 13:19.*
a) What was uppermost in Joseph's mind just before he died (see also Heb. 11:22)?
b) How might these last words of Joseph have helped the tribes of Israel in the years that followed?

NOTES

As you think back over the life of Joseph, God is speaking to you, showing you truths about Himself and His ways, and about yourself and what He is looking for in your life. That is why He has included the story of Joseph in His Word.

God is still adding pages to His casebook. If you belong to Him, and your name is written in the Lamb's Book of Life (Phil. 4:3; Rev. 21:27) He is writing your life story right now. Think back over events that have happened in your life, and remember that God has been looking at your heart, your character, the real you, and how you have dealt with each situation. Whatever comes your way in the days ahead, God will be looking for the fruits of His Spirit in your life.

Here is a page from God's casebook written several years ago. It comes from Tanzania, East Africa, and is part of a letter from Canon Kasaano, an African pastor and evangelist.

'I thank Jesus that He has used me in His work. I have met many difficult trials. After I lived at Ngara for three years, some louts burnt down my house, then burnt down another, yet I did not burden the Church of Christ. My first wife was stricken ill for four years and went to be with the Lord and I was without a wife (something unknown in African culture) for three years, yet I did not inconvenience the Church or make difficulties for the brethren. A crazed rogue killed my four-year-old child with a spear. God's grace helped me and I persuaded the judge not to hang him.

During the years of my service my average monthly wage was £12.00 and even today I don't have £2.00 in the bank and this is a big trial. But I don't forsake the Lamb of God, I thank Jesus who has made me rich in accepting me to live in His light; in giving me a house, a vegetable plot and children; the Diocese farewelling me with two cows.

In God's dealings with me He has always set my paths straight.'

(Quoted from the CMS Magazine *Contact*)

When you come to the end of your life, will you be able to say, with John Newton –

'Through many dangers, toils and snares
I have already come,
Tis Grace hath brought me safe thus far,
And Grace will lead me home.'

STUDY 11
EXTRA!

This may be used as an extra week's study, or may be done during holiday time with your family.

Joseph is a type of Jesus, who was to come later, and many interesting parallels may be seen in their lives. Look up each reference and note down any similarities between the corresponding one on the same line.

Genesis 30:23	John 1:29
Genesis 37:3	John 15:9
Acts 7:9	Matthew 27:18
Genesis 37:28; 39:1	Matthew 26:15; Philippians 2:7
Genesis 39:2, 21	Hebrews 5:8
Genesis 39:7-9	Matthew 4:8-10
Genesis 39:19-20	Acts 8:33; Matthew 26:63-67
Genesis 40:4	John 13:4-5
Genesis 41:40-43	Philippians 2:9-11
Genesis 45:7	John 3:17
Genesis 50:16-21	Luke 23:34

BOOK YOUR NEXT ORDER NOW!

ANSWER GUIDE

The following pages contain an Answer Guide. It is recommended that answers to the questions be attempted before turning to this guide. It is only a guide and the answers given should not be treated as exhaustive.

GUIDE TO INTRODUCTORY STUDY

The aim of this first day together is to discuss contemporary problems with the group, and then to see the parallel with the life of Joseph. From this should emerge the key to solving our own problems, large or small, or the problems of others we may be called upon to counsel.

With your particular group, how can you best help the members to put themselves in the shoes of the enquirers, and think out the answers with the help of God's Word? Our suggestion is that you divide the group into pairs or threes and give them each a problem, or assign a letter to each individual if the class is small.

Give each group a copy of the corresponding Scripture references listed below. Allow ten minutes, come together and let each group report their findings, giving time for comments. Watch the time as there must be at least twenty minutes reserved for looking into 'parallels' in the life of Joseph.

As leader, you should prepare thoughtfully for this Introductory Study, and pray that God will use it to meet real needs, either now or in the future. Be ready to guide discussion to Bible references. Have them at your fingertips.

Scripture references which will start us thinking along the line of God's answers

Problem 1	Proverbs 3:5-6; Psalm 119:25; Romans 8:28; Romans 5:5; Hosea 3:1.
Problem 2	James 4:7; 1 Corinthians 10:12-13; Proverbs 4:23; Matthew 15:19; Thessalonians 4:3-4.
Problem 3	Psalm 37:5-8; Psalm 73:23-26; Psalm 27:14; Psalm 34:1-4; 1 Peter 5:7.
Problem 4	Matthew 6:33; Deuteronomy 6:4-12; Psalm 139:23-24; Hebrews 10:25.
Problem 5	Matthew 5:23-24; Colossians 3:13; 1 Corinthians 13:4-5; Matthew 6:14-15; Hebrews 12:15.

GUIDE TO STUDY 1

DAY 1   Rachel m Jacob, Benjamin

DAY 2   a) Abraham m Sarah, Isaac m Rebekah, Esau
b) Reuben, Simeon, Levi, Judah, Issachar, Zebulon, Dan, Naphtali, Gad, Asher.

DAY 3   a) Desperately anxious for a son, frustrated, jealous of Leah.
b) Probably wildly happy with her new son and cleared of the stigma of not having children.
c) He could have become very spoiled?

DAY 4   a) The fear of Esau in the camp. His father Jacob's attitude of panic, then prayer and trust in God. His father limping after a tremendous experience with God.
b) Israel.

DAY 5   a) He ran to meet Jacob and embraced him with great joy.
b) Outside the city of Shechem.

DAY 6   a) His mother died as Benjamin was born.
b) At Mamre (Hebron), the home of Isaac.

DAY 7   a) Personal.
b) From very different backgrounds and lifestyles, one can be sinful and the other religious. Joseph must have been instructed about God although his family background was not perfect.

GUIDE TO STUDY 2

DAY 1 a) Joseph was his favourite, and he spoiled him. He was disturbed by the dream. He was desolate and inconsolable when he heard of Joseph's supposed death.
b) Yes. The need to avoid favouritism.

DAY 2 a) Genesis 37:4, 5, 11.
b) Personal. Recognise it as sin and contrary to God's Word, confess it to the Lord, pray for that person's good.

DAY 3 a) Dan, Naphtali, Gad and Asher.
b) Joseph had reported to his father some of the bad things they were doing. Perhaps they still felt aggrieved at being the first exposed to danger when meeting Esau.

DAY 4 a) They were men of violence, fierce, cruel and murderers.
b) Genesis 37:20.

DAY 5 a) He was Jacob's first-born and should have been the favoured one.
b) He prevented the others killing him. He would have rescued him and brought him back to his father.

DAY 6 a) He had the idea of selling him instead of letting him starve to death.
b) The Messiah, or Promised One would be born of the tribe of Judah.

DAY 7 a) 17.
b) conceited, fearful, or pleased to obey his father terrified, miserable.

GUIDE TO STUDY 3

DAY 1
a) The Lord was with Joseph.
b) God rescued him from all his troubles. He prospered. God gave him success in everything he did. He was granted favour in the eyes of the prison warden. He was given success in everything he did.

DAY 2
a) Joseph was doing his work to the glory of God, and God prospered him.
b) Personal.

DAY 3
a) Verse 10.
b) It would be to sin against God.
c) In Proverbs, the young man gives in to temptation.

DAY 4
a) By the power of God's Spirit dwelling within him. Also, he recognised that to give in would be sin against God.
b) Personal. (Read these verses, ask God's help and strength to overcome, get out of the way of temptation.)

DAY 5
a) She lied about Joseph and made false accusations against him.
b) Personal. An evil tongue can cause a lot of harm and distress.

DAY 6
a) One of patient endurance with the realisation that we have God's approval.
b) He was successful in all he did.

DAY 7
a) Personal; perhaps His silence.
b) If we think of His silence then this should teach us to think before we speak, and to trust God in every situation.

GUIDE TO STUDY 4

DAY 1 a) That God was with Joseph, even in prison.
b) He had the entire administration of the prison; all prisoners were responsible to him, and he had to wait on (at least) the two new prisoners who came in.

DAY 2 a) He asked him to remind Pharaoh that he was still in prison, and to ask him to let him out.
b) Both were able to help and minister to others.

DAY 3 a) Hope, excitement, thankfulness to God, and pity for the baker. Disillusioned, miserable, utterly wretched. (Note that Joseph never lost his faith in God.)
b) Wait silently and patiently for God.

DAY 4 a) These dreams must be interpreted by His people. To His own people He can communicate directly.
b) Through His Word, other people, conscience, a realisation of what He is saying when we pray and listen for His answer.

DAY 5 a) Pharaoh's dream, his concern, and the fact that the magicians couldn't (and didn't even attempt to) explain what it meant.
b) Seven fat cows came out of the river, then seven thin ones. The thin ones devoured the fat ones.

DAY 6 a) Yes, He could.
b) Because God's timing was perfect, and this was the time which fitted His plan (Gal. 4:4).

DAY 7 a) The seven fat cows (and ears) showed that there would be seven years of plenty in Egypt. The seven thin ones foretold famine.
b) Ultimately, to save His people (Jacob and his tribe) from starvation, and then to show His great power in delivering them from Egypt.

JOSEPH • ANSWER GUIDE

GUIDE TO STUDY 5

DAY 1 a) He is sovereign, and sustains the world. He sends or withholds the rain and growth.
b) Appoint people to be responsible for the storage grain during the seven good years.

DAY 2 a) Because he had shown himself to have a supernatural wisdom.
b) Personal.

DAY 3 a) The Christians in the early church considered all tasks to be important. Also because of Acts 6:1, they needed the wisdom that comes from God.
b) Personal.

DAY 4 a) The Prodigal Son (Luke 15). Some may suggest the exaltation of Christ.
b) Joseph had been careful to put God first in every situation to date, and God was now honouring His promise.

DAY 5 a) It might have made him proud, arrogant, self-centred and it might have caused him to forget God – but it didn't! Note that Jesus was this age (30) when He began his earthly ministry.
b) Personal.

DAY 6 a) A wife and two sons.
b) That they would share in his inheritance. (Note that when the Promised Land was divided among the tribes of Israel, large areas were assigned to Ephraim and Manasseh.) Bring a map of Canaan divided into tribes, if possible (Joshua chs. 13, 16, 17).

DAY 7 a) He gives them more responsibilities for Him.
b) Both were to be obeyed (Gen. 41:55; John 2:5). Hungry people were fed by Joseph and also by the Lord Jesus. Joseph was only able to satisfy the physical needs, Jesus the spiritual.

GUIDE TO STUDY 6

DAY 1   a) Personal.
b) What had happened in Genesis 37:25-28.

DAY 2   a) The father not allowing Benjamin to go with them; arrival in Egypt; the rough treatment from the governor; the mention of the brother who was dead.
b) He seems harsh, cruel and awe-inspiring.

DAY 3   a) Dread of having to ask father that Benjamin should come; fear of being the only one to return home, and later, fear of being the one to stay in prison. Discomfort and hurt pride at being put in prison, etc. (Three days in prison would give plenty of time to think!)
b) Verse 18. This Egyptian said he was a God-fearing man.

DAY 4   a) Genesis 42:21.
b) Reuben had been the one who tried to stop them getting rid of Joseph. (Leaders might look up the story of Genesis chapter 34, which gives an insight into the character of Simeon.)

DAY 5   a) The money found in the sacks.
b) God is punishing us (42:28).

DAY 6   a) He is terribly upset and against it.
b) Because Benjamin is the only son of Rachel still alive.

DAY 7   a) Benjamin has to go if more food is to be got. Failure to go will result in starvation. Judah guarantees personal protection of Benjamin. Time is being wasted and there is no alternative to going.
b) Genesis 43:14; that God would have mercy on them all and protect them.

GUIDE TO STUDY 7

DAY 1   a) Personal.
b) Joseph: overjoyed at the sight of Benjamin and wanting to show his love for them all by giving a feast. The brothers: suspicious, badly frightened, guilty.

DAY 2   a) In prison. Probably very relieved to find they had returned, and delighted to have his freedom again.
b) Those mentioned in chapter 43:11. What might look like a pitiful little offering of balm, oil and nuts, to a wealthy man of Egypt, represented so much from the famine-stricken land of Canaan.

DAY 3   a) Personal.
b) Joseph met Benjamin face to face and was overcome with emotion. Benjamin was seated at the lowest place at the feast (being the youngest), but was served five times as much food as the others – a token of honour. (Note that to men from a famine area, the banquet would be doubly impressive.)

DAY 4   a) He had his own silver cup put in Benjamin's sack, then sent his steward along to search for the cup, thus trying to prove Benjamin guilty of stealing it.
b) The plan was staged to test the brothers' attitude of heart – particularly to Benjamin.

DAY 5   a) They were so certain that they were all innocent.
b) That God was punishing them for their sins.

DAY 6   a) To see if they would be content to sacrifice Benjamin for their own safety. Remember how easily they got rid of Joseph years earlier, so that he wouldn't irritate them?
b) Judah was concerned for himself (that he wouldn't have a guilty conscience) in chapter 37, while in chapter 44 he is concerned for his father, and possibly Benjamin.

DAY 7   a) Yes. That the brothers (Judah being the spokesman) had had a real change of heart, and were really concerned about causing grief to their father.
b) Judah was prepared to suffer to allow Benjamin go free. Jesus sacrificed Himself for us.

GUIDE TO STUDY 8

DAY 1   a) Overwhelming love for those who don't deserve it.
b) Identification. Neither Joseph nor Jesus were ashamed to claim as brothers those who had sinned.

DAY 2   a) There was no bitterness or reproach where it might have seem justified.
b) Joseph showed a forgiving spirit to his brothers.

DAY 3   a) He had a certainty that God was in control.
b) Personal.

DAY 4   a) A practical concern for others.
b) He told his brothers to go and get their father and all their families and come to Egypt. He would take care of them in Egypt.

DAY 5   a) He had God's guidance in what he did, and this was confirmed by Pharaoh's suggestion.
b) Personal.

DAY 6   a) Carts full of provisions, new clothes, money and donkey-loads of food. This was an act of generosity born of love.
b) The messages they brought and the carts filled with food.

DAY 7   a) All of them.
b) Because the Holy Spirit controlled his life and he had 'crucified the sinful nature' (Gal. 5:24). He had been willing to submit his natural desires to God and to be obedient to His will. Suffering had refined him.

GUIDE TO STUDY 9

DAY 1 a) When he came to Beersheba, a sacred place for his father Isaac (Gen. 26:23-25), God appeared to Him after he had offered sacrifices. God gave him the assurance that this was in His plan and that he wasn't to be afraid. God said he would bring his descendants back to Canaan.
b) 75

DAY 2 a) Genesis 46:34. Shepherds were despised by the Egyptians.
b) The land of Goshen. (Bring a map.)

DAY 3 a) He blessed Pharaoh. (It was as if the grand old man Jacob (or Israel), the Patriarch, was granting Pharaoh an audience. Remember he was God's representative.)
b) Money. Livestock. Land. Themselves.

DAY 4 a) It was over. People are again planting grain.
b) He believed God's promise that His people would return there. Perhaps this was one way to encourage his sons to believe it too.

DAY 5 a) That God would multiply his descendants and give them the land of Canaan. (Notice in verse 5 that Joseph would have a double portion, as both his sons were to be inheritors and leaders of tribes.)
b) Personal.

DAY 6 a) Ephraim.
b) He put his right hand (the greater blessing) on Ephraim's head.
c) The promise to Joseph was fulfilled.

DAY 7 a) Abraham.
b) Psalm 105:24-25. The Egyptians hated and enslaved them.

GUIDE TO STUDY 10

DAY 1   a) Reuben, Simeon, Levi, Judah, Zebulun and Issachar.
b) The 'sceptre' indicates a king, and this is a prophecy. First, King David, and then later the King of Kings, the Lord Jesus, would come from the tribe of Judah.

DAY 2   a) Dan, Gad, Asher, Naphtali, Joseph and Benjamin.
b) Joseph comments on his fruitfulness, afflictions and faithfulness. God had helped and blessed him.

DAY 3   a) He prays that God will bless him richly with blessings of children, prosperity and plenty.
b) Every blessing of heaven! Redemption through the blood of Jesus, forgiveness of sins, and grace (unmerited favour and love).

DAY 4   Mentally alert, having a sense of accomplishment, and above all, peaceful, and at rest in the knowledge that God was with him in death as he had been in life.

DAY 5   a) A great number of Pharaoh's counsellors and assistants, all the senior officers of the land, all Joseph's brothers and their families (apart from small children).
b) When he was 17 and had been sold as a slave.

DAY 6   a) Because he realised that his brothers thought he had never really forgiven them, and was waiting to take his revenge.
b) The crucifixion of the Lord Jesus is the supreme example. Others are:
– Pharaoh (in Moses' day) not letting the people go, thus giving opportunity for God to demonstrate His power.
– Daniel thrown into the lions' den, and the subsequent decree that God should be worshipped in the land (Dan. 6:25-27).
– Stephen's death and the persecution of the early church, resulting in the spread of the Good News (Acts 8:4).
– etc., etc., God delights to turn evil into good!

DAY 7   a) That God would fulfil His promise and bring the nation back to the land He had given them (Gen. 15:13-14).
b) As they thought of his words, they would be inspired and encouraged by his faith to wait patiently for God to fulfil His promise.

JOSEPH • ANSWER GUIDE

THE WORD WORLDWIDE

We first heard of WORD WORLDWIDE over 20 years ago when Marie Dinnen, its founder, shared excitedly about the wonderful way ministry to a needy woman had exploded to touch many lives. It was great to see the Word of God being made central in the lives of thousands of men and women, then the life changing effects that resulted when they applied the Word into their circumstances. Over the years the vision for WORD WORLDWIDE has not dimmed in the hearts of those who are involved in this ministry. God is still at work through His Word and in today's self-seeking society, the Word is even more relevant to those who desire true meaning and purpose in life. WORD WORLDWIDE is a ministry of WEC International, an interdenominational missionary society, whose sole purpose for existence is to see Christ known, loved and worshipped by all, particularly those who have yet to hear of His wonderful name. This ministry is a vital part of our work and we warmly recommend the WORD WORLDWIDE 'Geared for Growth' Bible studies to you. We know that as you study His Word you will be enriched in your personal walk with Christ. It is our hope that as you are blessed through these studies, you will find opportunities to help others find a personal relationship with Jesus. As a mission we would encourage you to work with us to make Christ known to the ends of the earth.

Stewart and Jean Moulds – British Directors, **WEC International**.

A full list of over 50 'Geared for Growth' studies can be obtained from:

ENGLAND John and Ann Edwards
5 Louvain Terrace, Hetton-le Hole, Tyne & Wear, DH5 9PP
Tel. 0191 5262803   Email: rhysjohn.edwards@virgin.net

IRELAND Steffney Preston
33 Harcourts Hill, Portadown, Craigavon, N. Ireland, BT62 3RE
Tel. 028 3833 7844 Email: sa.preston@talk21.com

SCOTLAND Margaret Halliday
10 Douglas Drive, Newton Mearns, Glasgow, G77 6HR
Tel. 0141 639 8695 Email: m.halliday@ntlworld.com

WALES William and Eirian Edwards
Penlan Uchaf, Carmarthen Road, Kidwelly, Carms., SA17 5AF
Tel. 01554 890423 Email: Penlan.uchaf@farming.co.uk

UK CO-ORDINATOR
Anne Jenkins, 2 Windermere Road, Carnforth, Lancs., LA5 9AR
Tel. 01524 734797 Email: anne@jenkins.abelgratis.com

www.wordworldwide.org.uk

Christian Focus Publications publishes biblically-accurate books for adults and children. The books in the adult range are published in three imprints.

Christian Heritage contains classic writings from the past.

Christian Focus contains popular works including biographies, commentaries, doctrine, and Christian living.

Mentor focuses on books written at a level suitable for Bible College and seminary students, pastors, and others; the imprint includes commentaries, doctrinal studies, examination of current issues, and church history.

For a free catalogue of all our titles, please write to the address below.

ISBN 0 90806 700 3

Copyright © WEC International

Published in 2002 by
Christian Focus Publications, Geanies House,
Fearn, Ross-shire, IV20 ITW, Scotland
and
WEC International, Bulstrode, Oxford Road,
Gerrards Cross, Bucks , SL9 8SZ

www.christianfocus.com

Cover design by Alister MacInnes

Printed and bound by Bell and Bain